If I Were a Cricket...

If I Were a Cricket...

BY KAZUE MIZUMURA

Thomas Y. Crowell Company   New York

BY THE AUTHOR:

The Blue Whale
The Emperor Penguins
If I Built a Village...
If I Were a Cricket...
If I Were a Mother...
I See the Winds
The Way of an Ant

Manufactured in the United States of America
CIP Card
ISBN 0-690-00075-8
    0-690-00076-6   (LB)

    2   3   4   5   6   7   8   9   10

To
Naomi

If I were a cricket,
all through the autumn nights
I would sing
for you,
a silver bell song
you would
never forget.

If I were a snail
carrying my house
on my back in the rain,
I would move
next door to you,
so I could see you
every day.

If I were a ladybug,
shiny as a ruby,
I would sit very very still
on your finger,
and hope to become
your favorite ring.

If I were a turtle,
I would crawl slowly
and even stop
now and then,
to make sure
you would always
win the race
with me.

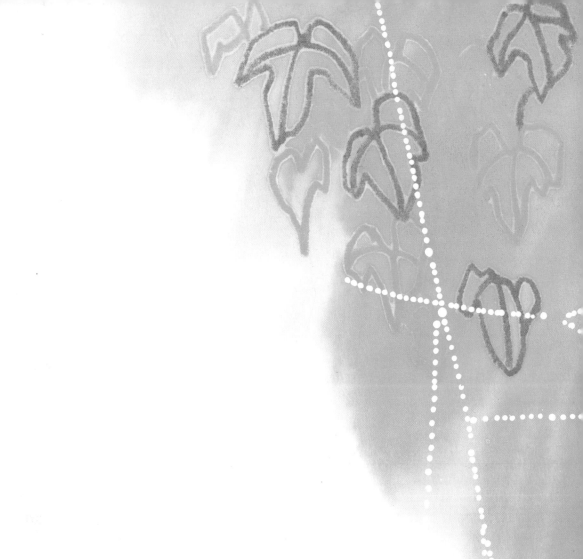

If I were a spider,
on a summer morning,
I would string
the sparkling dew
in my web,
and catch the rising sun
for you.

If I were a frog,
on a water lily,
and I saw you
at the edge of the pond,
I would leap
with joy,
and plunge into your shadow
in the water.

If I were a firefly,
high and low
I would glow in the night,
and when you are near me,
I would fill
your cupped hands
with my golden light.

If I were a bee,
gathering nectars
from the roses in your garden,
I would invite you
to my comb
for honey,
if you would follow me.

If I were a lizard,
slipping in and out
of the rocks,
I would play
hide-and-seek with you
all day long.

If I were an oyster,
pretending to be a rock
on the reef,
and you came
looking for me,
I would surprise you
with a gift of a pearl.

If I were a dragonfly,
shimmering my wings
against the setting sun,
like a helicopter,
I would carry your wish
to the first evening star,
to make it come true.

If I were a starfish
washed ashore on the beach,
I would wait
until you found me,
hoping to be
the star,
on top of your
Christmas tree.

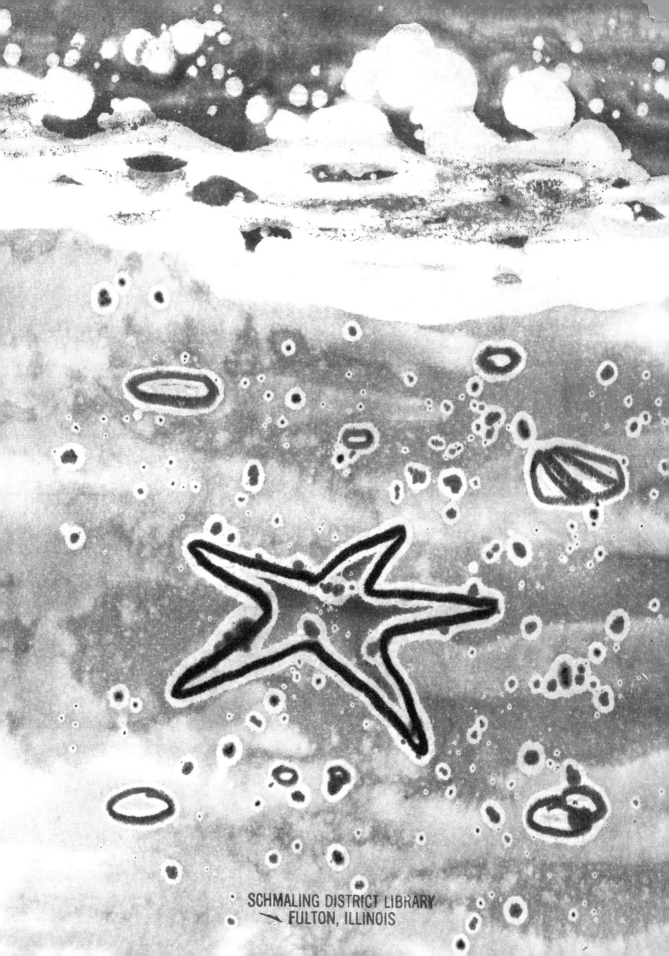

There are many ways
to say that
I love you,
But I just smile
to let you know that
I do.

About the Author

Kazue Mizumura has long been interested in the world of nature, and this concern is evident in all her books. Miss Mizumura is both author and illustrator of a number of distinguished picture books for children, including THE WAY OF AN ANT, I SEE THE WINDS (an A.L.A. Notable book), IF I WERE A MOTHER . . . (an A.L.A. Notable Book), and IF I BUILT A VILLAGE . . . (First Prize, Boston Globe—Horn Book Award, 1971).

Miss Mizumura was born in Kamakura, Japan, and now lives in Stamford, Connecticut. She studied at the Women's Art Institute in Tokyo, as well as at Pratt Institute in Brooklyn, New York. In addition to writing and illustrating books, her busy life includes the making of ceramics and jewelry, for she believes firmly in the importance of handicrafts.